KIKAR'S D

Olivia Bennett

Photographs by Christopher Cormack

Hamish Hamilton
London

'Keep still so that I can finish your plait,' says Pujenay to her little sister Kuljeet.
'We are going on a shopping expedition to Southall this morning. Dad is going to buy a drum for Kikar.'

Kikar is their brother. He is twelve years old. They have two other brothers. There is Butta, who is nine and a half, and Munjeet. He is three and a half. Munjeet's family are Sikhs but he is too young to wear a turban like his brothers. Mum tidies his hair into a small knot and covers it with a square piece of cloth called a patka.

The Singh family live in east London. It will take Dad nearly an hour to drive to Southall, but he knows they will find several shops there selling Indian musical instruments. The one Kikar wants is a hand drum.

As soon they arrive in Southall, Kikar and Butta want to buy the drum. But the first shop they pass is a store selling saris and lengths of material. 'We must go in here first,' says Mum. 'I want to look at materials for Pujenay.'

Pujenay is eighteen. She is getting married next year. Mum is making her some beautiful saris for the wedding ceremony and the celebrations afterwards. They find some material just like one of the saris Mum has already made so they buy a blouse to match.

'See if you can find anything you like here, Kuljeet,' says Mum. She is making Kuljeet a new outfit too. Kuljeet's favourite colour is blue.

They leave the materials shop and walk on down the High Street.
'Now we will get the drum,' thinks Kikar.
But just then they pass a jewellery shop.
'Look at those necklaces, Mum,' says Pujenay.

Over the last six months her mother and father have been buying
her the pieces of gold jewellery she needs for her marriage. By the
time the wedding takes place Pujenay will have a complete
collection of gold hairclips, earrings, bracelets, necklaces and rings,
just like her Mum did when she got married.

'How does this look?'

Pujenay's parents look at several pieces of jewellery but they decide not to buy anything today.

While Pujenay and her parents are talking to the jeweller, Kikar and Butta look through the window of the shop next door. 'There's a film being shown on the TV inside the shop,' says Kikar.

'I've seen it before,' replies Butta.

At last the others come out of the jeweller's. Butta sees a shop selling records and musical instruments but they have hardly any drums. Outside the shop is a stall selling coloured and tinsel bracelets. These are called rakhi.

'This is lucky,' says Mum. 'Pujenay, Kuljeet and I need to buy some for the festival of Raksha Bandan next week.' Raksha Bandan is a Hindu festival. On that day, sisters tie a rakhi onto their brothers' wrists.

The rakhi is a sign of affection between brother and sister. When a girl ties one onto her brother's wrist, it means she trusts him to protect and look after her. In return, the brother often gives a small present. This is usually money.

Although Raksha Bandan is a Hindu festival, it is celebrated by many Indians, whatever their religion. Many Sikh families follow the custom of giving rakhi. Mum always sends some to her two brothers in Cardiff in time for Raksha Bandan. Dad's three sisters usually visit him for the festival and bring rakhi for him. Daughters can give fathers rakhi too. Last year Dad had five on his arm!

There are lots of different kinds of rakhi on the stall. Kuljeet has a lovely time choosing some to give to her brothers and father.

At last Kikar and Butta are happy. The stallholder told them where to find the best musical instrument shop in Southall.

Inside there are rows and rows of drums. Some are made from wood, others are brightly painted and some are made of shiny metal. Underneath there are some harmoniums. The drums and harmoniums are played in Sikh temples during services and at ceremonies such as weddings. Kikar wants to be good enough to play at Pujenay's marriage celebrations.

Mum shows Kuljeet some
dancing bells. They are called
ghungroos.
'You attach the bracelet round
your ankle and the bells tinkle as
you move,' explains Mum.

On the wall behind them are
some sitars. They are beautifully
made and very expensive.

15

Meanwhile Kikar has chosen the drum he wants. One of the shop assistants shows him how to tune it. He explains how to loosen and tighten the screws which keep the skin stretched across the ends of the drum.

While Dad pays the shopkeeper, Kikar shows Munjeet what he has learnt. There are so many things to look at in the shop that the children do not want to leave.

There are cymbals, flutes, maracas, trumpets, bugles and many different kinds of drum. At last Mum persuades them to come away. 'It's nearly lunchtime,' she says.

Everyone is hungry by the time they get home. Mum quickly heats up the chicken and chips she has cooked for lunch.
'Can I have some tomato ketchup, please?' asks Butta.
'I prefer vinegar on my chips,' says Kuljeet.

After lunch Pujenay shows Kuljeet some of the jewellery and other gifts Mum and Dad have bought for her. In her bedroom there is a large metal trunk filled with all the things she will need to set up her new home. There are pillowcases, blankets, a tea set, plates, pots and pans and some embroidered material for her saris.

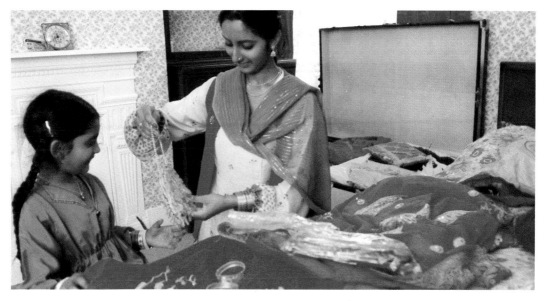

Meanwhile Butta helps Munjeet with his reading. They look at an alphabet book.
Munjeet loves books and his brothers and sisters are always happy to help him.

Mum takes advantage of the peace and quiet to write to her family in Cardiff. She puts some rakhi in the envelopes so that her brothers will get them in time for Raksha Bandan next week.

Later in the afternoon the family go to the Sikh temple in Bow, east London. A Sikh temple is called a gurdwara. Mr Singh has asked the priest there if he will give Kikar and Butta a few lessons on the drum.

On the way to the temple, they post Mum's letters. When they arrive, Mum, Pujenay and Kuljeet pull their scarves, which are called dupattas, over their heads. Women and girls must always cover their heads before they enter the prayer room.

Everyone takes off their shoes in the temple porch and they go inside. The priest, who is called a granthi, is waiting for them. He is reading the holy book of the Sikhs. This is called the Guru Granth Sahib. It lies on a raised platform and is covered with an embroidered canopy. The Guru Granth Sahib is very precious to Sikhs. No ceremony such as a wedding is complete unless it takes place in the presence of the holy book.

'I don't think I've ever seen the gurdwara this empty,' whispers Kuljeet to Butta. Usually the family visits the temple for a service, when it is full of people.

22

The first thing the Singhs do is to kneel and bow down in front of the holy book. They make an offering to the gurdwara funds.

The granthi looks after the Guru Granth Sahib and reads from it during services. Dad, Kikar and Butta chat to him for a while. Kikar explains that he wants to be good enough to play at Pujenay's wedding celebrations.

The granthi sits down with Kikar and Butta on the platform where the temple musicians play. Singing the hymns in the Guru Granth Sahib is an important part of Sikh worship. He shows Kikar and Butta how to use their fingers to get different sounds out of the drum. He tells Kikar to practise this before his next lesson.

'You can make the sound higher by tightening the drum skin, but be careful not to overstretch it by turning the screws too hard.'

When they get home from the temple, they play a game called Pasha. It is a bit like Ludo. They throw cowrie shells instead of dice. The more shells you throw which land the right way up, the more moves you can make.

'Pujenay always seem to win!'
says Butta.
'Never mind, Butta,' says
Kuljeet. 'Supper is ready. Mum
has made pakora and samosa
for us.'

After supper Kikar goes off to
the boys' bedroom. He can't
resist a last practise on his drum!
'I really think I'm getting the
hang of it now. I'm sure I'll be
good enough to play at
Pujenay's wedding.'